[Office 101]

» an illustrated guide

» **Geoffrey Day-Lewis**

Andrews McMeel
Publishing, LLC

Kansas City

#1 [Look forward to Mondays.]

#2 [Dress to impress.]

#3 [Time is money.]

#4 [Be a communicator.]

#5 [Learn to follow instructions.]

#6 [Stay hydrated.]

#7 [Make technology your friend.]

#8 [Make your work space a sanctuary.]

#9 [Don't take shortcuts.]

#10 [Don't be afraid to express yourself.]

#11 [Embrace new challenges.]

#12

[Learn to prioritize.]

#13 [Many hands make light work.]

#14 [There's no "I" in team.]

#15 [Good work never goes unrewarded.]

#16!!!

[The customer is always right.]

#17 [The boss is always right too!]

#18 [Always give 100 percent]

MONDAY—2 percent

TUESDAY—13 percent

WEDNESDAY—29 percent

THURSDAY—21 percent

FRIDAY—35 percent

#19 [Believe in yourself.]

#20 [Honesty is the best policy.]

#21 [Learn to delegate.]

#22
[Be brave.]

#23 [Don't get carried away on casual Friday.]

#24 [Be a team player.]

#25 [Everyone makes mistakes.]

#27 [If at first you don't succeed...

destroy all evidence that you tried.]

#28 [Don't gossip.]

#29 [Be flexible.]

#30 [Keep cool.]

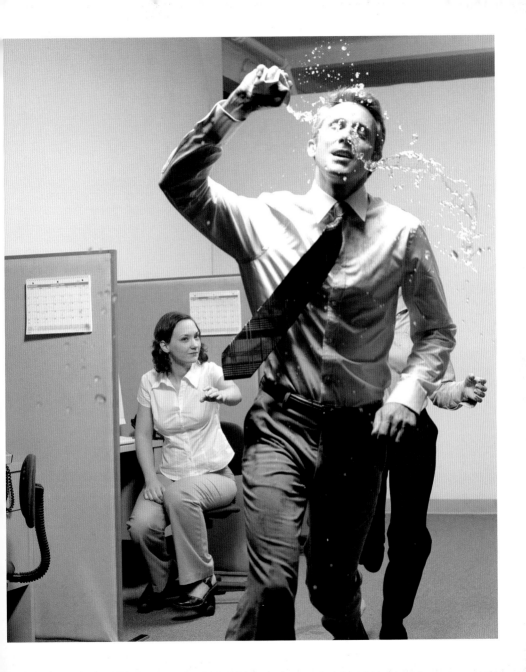

#31 [Think before you act.]

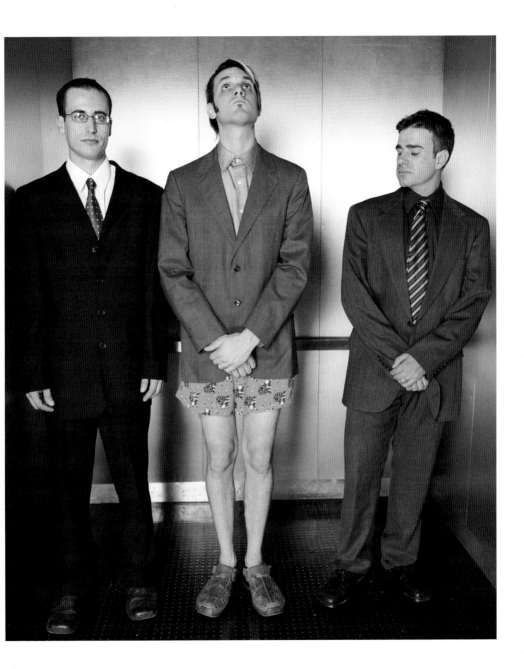

#32 [Keep an active imagination.]

#33 [Sometimes it takes guts.]

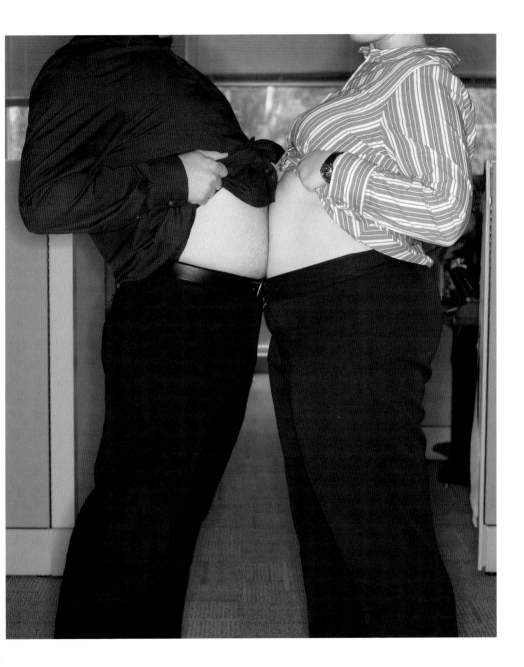

#34
[If you can keep your head
when all about you are losing theirs...

**it's quite possible
you haven't grasped the situation.]**

#35 [Keep an even temper.]

#36 [Stay focused.]

#37 [If all else fails, try to look busy.]

#38 [Play hard, work hard.]

#39
[When you are in it up to your ears,
it pays to keep your mouth shut.]

#40 [Practice makes perfect.]

#41
[Be a listener.]

#42

[Pay attention to detail.]

#43 [Haste makes waste.]

#44 [Don't be afraid to ask for help.]

cheeky cheeky cheeky cheeky cheeky cheeky cheeky
cheeky cheeky cheeky cheeky cheeky cheeky cheeky
cheeky cheeky cheeky cheeky cheeky cheeky cheeky
cheeky cheeky cheeky cheeky cheeky cheeky cheeky
cheeky cheeky cheeky cheeky cheeky cheeky cheeky
cheeky cheeky cheeky cheeky cheeky cheeky cheeky
cheeky cheeky cheeky cheeky cheeky cheeky cheeky
cheeky cheeky cheeky cheeky cheeky cheeky cheeky

#45 [Respect company equipment.]

cheeky cheeky cheeky cheeky cheeky cheeky cheeky
cheeky cheeky cheeky cheeky cheeky cheeky cheeky
cheeky cheeky cheeky cheeky cheeky cheeky cheeky
cheeky cheeky cheeky cheeky cheeky cheeky cheeky
cheeky cheeky cheeky cheeky cheeky cheeky cheeky
cheeky cheeky cheeky cheeky cheeky cheeky cheeky
cheeky cheeky cheeky cheeky cheeky cheeky cheeky
cheeky cheeky cheeky cheeky cheeky cheeky cheeky

#46

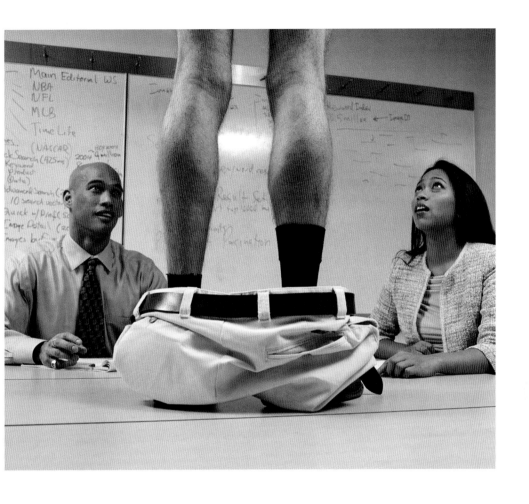

[Learn how to make friends and influence people.]

#47 [Don't shoot the messenger.]

#48 [Always lend a hand.]

#49

[Keep

a tidy

work space!]

#50
[Try to behave at the Christmas party.]

#51 [♥]

#52 [♥] #53 [♥]

#54 [♥] #55 [♥] #56 [♥]

#57 [♥] #58 [♥] #59 [♥] #60 [♥]

#61 [♥] #62 [♥] #63 [♥] #64 [♥] #65 [♥]

#66 [♥] #67 [♥] #68 [♥] #69 [♥] #70 [♥] #71 [♥]

#72 [♥] #73 [♥] #74 [♥] #75 [♥] #76 [♥] #77 [♥] #78 [♥]

#79 [♥] #80 [♥] #81 [♥] #82 [♥] #83 [♥] #84 [♥]

#85 [♥] #86 [♥] #87 [♥] #88 [♥] #89 [♥]

#90 [♥] #91 [♥] #92 [♥] #93 [♥]

#94 [♥] #95 [♥] #96 [♥]

#97 [♥] #98 [♥]

#99 [♥]

[The key to success is to LOVE YOUR WORK!]

#100
[Never give up.]

#101 [The possibilities are infinite.]

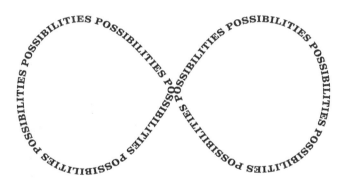

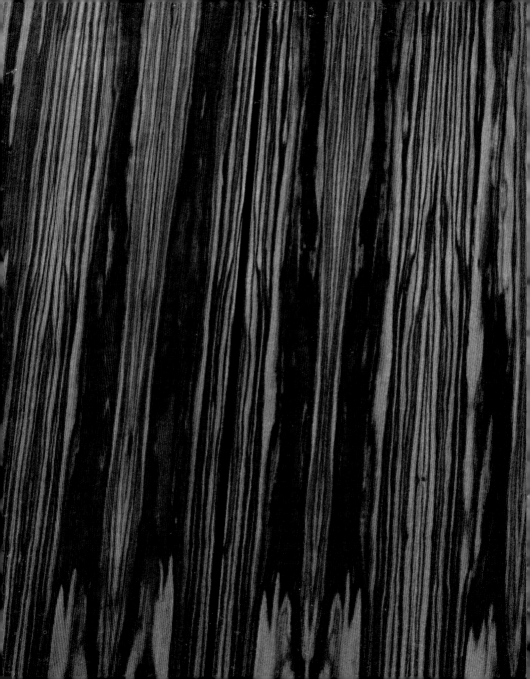